2 - 66

BOOKS BY WILLIAM MEREDITH

The Cheer   1980
Hazard, the Painter   1975
Earth Walk: New and Selected Poems   1970
The Wreck of the Thresher and Other Poems   1964
The Open Sea and Other Poems   1958
Ships and Other Figures   1948
Love Letter from an Impossible Land   1944

TRANSLATED BY WILLIAM MEREDITH
Alcools: Poems 1898–1913 by Guillaume Apollinaire   1964

EDITED BY WILLIAM MEREDITH
Shelley: Selected Poems   1962

The Cheer

WILLIAM
MEREDITH

The Cheer

Alfred A. Knopf
New York
1980

Copyright © 1971, 1972, 1974, 1975, 1976, 1977, 1978, 1979, 1980 by William
Meredith

"At the Confluence of the Colorado," "Country Stars," "Dying Away," Memoirs,"
"Parents," and "Winter on the River" were originally published in The New Yorker.
"Crossing Over" was originally published in Georgia Review.
"Here and There" was originally published by R. H. Deutsch, The Wallace
Stevens Journal.
"Not Both" was first published as a broadside by Palaemon Press Limited.
"Recollection of Bellagio" was originally published in Thoughts From the Lake of
Time, the Josiah Macy, Jr. Foundation.
"My Mother's Life" and "The Revenant" were originally published in Poetry.
Other poems have been previously published by the Folger Shakespeare Library,
New Letters, New Republic, Poet Lore, Pomegranate Press, Saturday Review,
and the Washington Post.

Grateful acknowledgment is made to the following for permission to reprint from
previously published material:
Alfred A. Knopf, Inc.: "The Idea of Order at Key West" by Wallace Stevens.
Copyright 1936 by Wallace Stevens, renewed 1964 by Holly Stevens. Reprinted
from The Collected Poems of Wallace Stevens. Reprinted by permission of
Alfred A. Knopf, Inc.
Basic Books, Inc.: "The Interment of Nicolai Vasilich Gogol" by Andrei
Voznesensky. From Antiworlds and the Fifth Ace by Andrei Volznesensky, edited
by Patricia Blake and Max Hayward, copyright © 1966, 1967 by Basic Books, Inc.,
Publishers, New York, copyright © 1963 by Encounter Ltd.
Random House, Inc.: Excerpt from "Recollection in Upper Ontario, from Long
Ago" by Robert Penn Warren, from Being Here: Poetry 1977–1980 by Robert Penn
Warren. Copyright © 1978, 1979, 1980 by Robert Penn Warren. Reprinted by
permission of Random House, Inc.

Library of Congress Cataloging in Publication Data
Meredith, William, [date]
The cheer.
Poetry.
I. Title.
PS3525.E588C47   1980   811'.54   80-7649
ISBN O-394-51341-X

To Richard Harteis

Poems on the pages indicated are dedicated to friends and members of my family: Kolyo Sevov (5); John and Charlotte Marshall (8); Lee and Stewart Udall (20); Richard and Charlee Wilbur (26); In memory of Patricia Dionne Keyser, 1924–74 (27); Vanessa Meredith and Samuel Wolf Gezari (32); William and Emmy Maxwell (35); Harriet Skidmore Arnold (56); and Robert Penn Warren and Eleanor Clark (61).

The Cheer,

reader my friend, is in the words here, somewhere.
Frankly, I'd like to make you smile.
Words addressing evil won't turn evil back
but they can give heart.
The cheer is hidden in right words. ——

A great deal isn't right, as they say,
as they are lately at some pains to tell us.
Words have to speak about that.
They would be the less words
for saying *smile* when they should say *do*.
If you ask them *do what?*
they turn serious quick enough, but never unlovely. ——
And they will tell you what to do,
if you listen, if you want that.

Certainly good cheer has never been what's wrong,
though solemn people mistrust it.
Against evil, between evils, lovely words are right.
How absurd it would be to spin these noises out,
so serious that we call them poems,——
if they couldn't make a person smile.
Cheer or courage is what they were all born in.
It's what they're trying to tell us, miming like that.
It's native to the words,
and what they want us always to know,
even when it seems quite impossible to do.

CONTENTS

63

W˙R

MS,
FW
˙WH

A˙B

65

66

The Cheer

WINTER ON THE RIVER

dawn

A long orange knife slits the darkness
from ear to ear. Flat sheets of Kansas
have been dropped where the water was.
A blue snake is lying perfectly still,
freezing to avoid detection—no, it is the barge-road.

noon

It's six weeks past the solstice. What
is the sun thinking of? It skulks
above the southern woods at noon.
                                    Two ducks descend
on the thin creek that snakes through the plain of ice.
They dream of a great flood coming
to devastate this plastic geography.
We can all remember other things than snow.

dusk

At dusk the east bank glows a colder orange,
giving back heat reluctantly. (The sickle moon
gives it back quickly.) The snake is glacier-green
where an oil-barge has lately churned it.
Tonight unlucky creatures will die, like so many
soldiers or parents, it is nobody's fault.

3

midnight

The farm dogs bark at a soft crash far up-river:
the ice-breaker is coming down. We go out
in the clear night to see the lights—beacons
on the river, pharos in the sky, and a jewelled
seafarer bringing water to the parched plain.
The hollow roar grows slower than an avalanche.
Her search-light feeling a way from point
of land to point of land, she pulls herself along
by beacon-roots. For a half-mile reach of river
she sights on us, a group of goblins blinking
in front of their white house. Sugary rime
feathers from the bow. An emerald and a garnet
flank the twitching eye.
                    Abruptly she turns,
offering the beam of a ship that has nothing to do with us.
A houseful of strangers passes, ship-noise thumping.

Down-river, other dogs take up the work.
They are clearing a path for the barges of cold
and silence which the creatures are expecting.

4

TWO MASKS UNEARTHED
IN BULGARIA

When God was learning to draw the human face
I think he may have made a few like these
that now look up at us through museum glass
a few miles north of where they slept
for six thousand years, a necropolis near Varna.
With golden staves and ornaments around them
they lay among human bodies but had none.
Gods themselves, or soldiers lost abroad—
we don't know who they are.

The gold buttons which are their curious eyes,
the old clay which is their wrinkled skin,
seem to have been worked by the same free hand
that drew Adam for the Jews about that time.
It is moving, that the eyes are still questioning
and no sadder than they are, time being what it is—
as though they saw nothing tragic in the faces
looking down through glass into theirs.
Only clay and gold, they seem to say,
passing through one condition on its way to the next.

FREEZING

It is the normal excellence, of long accomplishment.

"The Abnormal Is Not Courage" / Jack Gilbert

i

When the shadow of the sparrowhawk passes over,
the small birds caught in the open, freeze.

ii

Surprised in the mowed grass
on his way back to the stone wall
in the cool of the late afternoon,
the blacksnake holds three curves
for as long as I bend to watch him.

iii

To know what is possible,
and to do that.

iv

In the dream, I lie still.
Booted and brutal,
their pieces slung at waist height
spraying random lead,

they wade through the dead
for one of whom I hope to be mistaken.
When I wake up, what am I to do
with this mortifying life I've saved again?

v

To live out our lives under a good tyrant
is a lot to ask, the old man said.
There are reports that the swaggering brothers
and their wives and foreign in-laws
are shouting again, in the marble house
that looks down on the harbor and the town.
We know what they are capable of,
quarreling with one another
and in contention with the gods.
We keep indoors.
Impatience and ignorance sometimes ignite
in a flash of bravery among us,
he said. It is usually inappropriate.

vi

Some normal excellence, of long accomplishment,
is all that can justify our sly survivals.

RECOLLECTION OF BELLAGIO

On the dark lake below, the fishermen's bells
are calling to one another from their nets.
Who is here on the dark promontory at night?
Tossed by the April wind,
a horizontal pine, warped to the cliff,
married to the limestone cliff by the east wind,
rises and falls, rises and falls.
And who sees, against the stars,
the needled tufts change and exchange
like dancers, gracious dependents?
The fixed stars are a commodious dancing-
floor, at any moment the pine-tufts
know where their home-places are
on the polished floor of the marble constellations.

How long has this been going on, this *allemande*,
before a man's thoughts climbed up to sit
on the limestone knob and watch (briefly,
as man's thoughts' eyes watch) the needles
keeping time to the bells which the same wind rocks
on the water below, marking the fishermen's nets—
thoughts he would haul in later from the lake
of time, feeling himself drawn clumsy
back into time's figure, hand over hand,
by the grace of pine boughs? And who
is saying these words, now that that man
is a shade, has become his own shade?
I see the shade rise slow and ghostly from its seat
on the soft, grainy stone, I watch it descend
by the gravelled paths of the promontory,

under a net of steady stars, in April,
from the boughs' rite and the bells'—quiet,
my shade, and long ago, and still going on.

COUNTRY STARS

The nearsighted child has taken off her glasses
and come downstairs to be kissed goodnight.
She blows on a black windowpane until it's white.
Over the apple trees a great bear passes
but she puts her own construction on the night.

Two cities, a chemical plant, and clotted cars
breathe our distrust of darkness on the air,
clouding the pane between us and the stars.
But have no fear, or only proper fear:
the bright watchers are still there.

HOMAGE TO PAUL MELLON, I. M. PEI, THEIR GALLERY, AND WASHINGTON CITY

Granite and marble,
women and men,
took a long while to make.

America and the Bill of Rights,
a lot of trouble,
and it's not done yet. Praise be.
It is so interesting,
and lucky, like crustacean deposit.

We've troubled the stones to stand up here
in attitudes of serenity,
our guesses at un-trouble,
what that must be like.
(These are short whiles,
to a stone's way of thinking.)

Meanwhile, Munch and Noguchi
and a long deposit of the sweetest troublers
required this reckless glacier,
these knives of stone, these pink prows,
and among them, safe hogans of white space.

And where would any of us be
if the limestone creatures had held back,
the roiling magma demurred? or the genes?
We've given assent to ourselves
in this city for a while,
laying down stone like our own sweet lives.

ON JENKINS' HILL

(the old name for Capitol Hill)

The weather came over this low knoll, west to east,
before there was a word for leaf-fall, before
there were any leaves. Weathers will nuzzle and preen
whatever earthwork we leave here. And we know now,
don't we, that we will be leaving, by fire or ice,
our own or His, or at the very worst, nobody's.
May that be a long time off. Now,
it is our hill for debating.

The dome at the top of the hill, heavy with reference,
is iron out of the soil, yearned up as if it were white stone,
the way for a time our thought and rhetoric yearned upward.
Here our surrogates sit. It is almost too much for them,
some days, to make the world go around.
They are urged to clean it, to sully it more grandly,
to let it alone. We have elected them, they are our elect.

If we only knew what to ask, there are trees, white oaks,
not far from here that have seen the whole thing.
Year after year they have put on new growth, dropped leaves.
I can tell you this much: it is a badly informed citizen
who stands on this hill and scoffs.

A FIRESCREEN AT
MOUNT VERNON

When the face is struck
by the nearer sun
in the fireplace,
summer or winter
the eyes water.

See in the painting
of the iron-works
how the ingot hurts—
the visitor cowers
like a bad angel,
arm over face,
the apprentice weeps.
All but the smithy,
toughened like Vulcan,
turn from the heat.

And here indoors
in the gentleroom
is a thin inflammable
furniture,
a wooden rack
(which you would think
in that final access
of reasonableness
they'd have wrought of iron).
It holds a small screen,
some woman's skill,
a needlepoint scene
between face and fire,

shading those faces
whose evenings are gone.

Erect of posture,
sociably garbed,
they were far from the smoke
of midden and cave,
as we are no longer
who marvel dry-eyed
and stare like savages
at this fragile decorum
of rosewood or fruitwood,
imagining people
whom reading or sewing
had fired to tears.

A MILD-SPOKEN CITIZEN
FINALLY WRITES TO THE
WHITE HOUSE

Please read this letter when you are alone.
Don't be afraid to listen to what may change you,
I am urging on you only what I myself have done.

In the first place, I respect the office, although one night
last spring, when you had committed (in my eyes)
criminal folly, and there was a toast to you, I wouldn't rise.

A man's mistakes (if I may lecture you), his worst acts,
aren't out of character, as he'd like to think,
are not put on him by power or stress or too much to drink,

but are simply a worse self he consents to be. Thus
there is no mistaking you. I marvel that there's
so much disrespect for a man just being himself, being his errors.

"I never met a worse man than myself,"
Thoreau said. When we're our best selves, we can all
afford to say that Self-respect is best when marginal.

And when the office of the presidency will again
accommodate that remark (Did you see? Fidel Castro
said almost that recently), it may be held by better men

than you or me. Meantime, I hear there is music in your house,
your women wear queens' wear, though winds howl outside,
and I say, that's all right, the man should have some ease,

but does anyone say to your face who you really are?
No, they say *Mr. President,* while any young person
feels free to call me *voter, believer,* even *causer.*

And if I were also a pray-er, a man given to praying,
(I'm often in fact careless about great things, like you)
and I wanted to pray for your office, as in fact I do,

the words that would come to me would more likely be
god change you than *god bless the presidency.*
I would pray, *God cause the President to change.*

As I myself have been changed, first my head, then my heart,
so that I no longer pretend that I don't swindle or kill
when there is swindling and killing on my nation's part.

Well. Go out into your upstairs hall tonight with this letter.
Generous ghosts must walk that house at night,
carrying draughts of the Republic like cold water

to a man parched after too much talk and wine and smoke.
Hear them. They are elected ghosts, though some will be radicals
and all may want to tell you things you will not like.

It will seem dark in the carpeted hall, despite the night-lights
in the dull sconces. Make the guard let you pass.
"If you are the President," a shade with a water-glass

will ask you (and this is all I ask), calling you by name,
himself perhaps a famous name, "If you are the President,
and things in the land have come to all this shame,

why don't you try doing something new? This building rose,
laborious as a dream, to house one character:
man trusting man anew. That's who each tenant is

—or an impostor, as some of us have been."

1969

ACCIDENTS OF BIRTH

Je vois les effroyables espaces de l'Univers qui m'enferment, et je me trouve attaché à un coin de cette vaste étendue, sans savoir pourquoi je suis plutôt en ce lieu qu'en un autre, ni pourquoi ce peu de temps qui m'est donné à vivre m'est assigné à ce point plutôt qu'à un autre de toute l'éternité qui m'a précédé, et de toute qui me suit.

Pensées sur la religion / Pascal

The approach of a man's life out of the past is history, and the approach of time out of the future is mystery. Their meeting is the present, and it is consciousness, the only time life is alive. The endless wonder of this meeting is what causes the mind, in its inward liberty of a frozen morning, to turn back and question and remember. The world is full of places. Why is it that I am here?

The Long-Legged House / *Wendell Berry*

Spared by a car- or airplane-crash or
cured of malignancy, people look
around with new eyes at a newly
praiseworthy world, blinking eyes like these.

For I've been brought back again from the
fine silt, the mud where our atoms lie
down for long naps. And I've also been
pardoned miraculously for years
by the lava of chance which runs down
the world's gullies, silting us back.
Here I am, brought back, set up, not yet
happened away.

                     But it's not this random
life only, throwing its sensual
astonishments upside down on
the bloody membranes behind my eyeballs,
not just me being here again, old
needer, looking for someone to need,
but you, up from the clay yourself,
as luck would have it, and inching
over the same little segment of earth-
ball, in the same little eon, to
meet in a room, alive in our skins,
and the whole galaxy gaping there
and the centuries whining like gnats—
you, to teach me to see it, to see
it with you, and to offer somebody
uncomprehending, impudent thanks.

AT THE CONFLUENCE OF
THE COLORADO AND
THE LITTLE COLORADO

Where the two rivers come together—one cold,
one desert-warm—the party beached the raft to swim.
A blue aileron, looking new, lay on the bank
and Dennis put his shirt and bluejeans in it,
out of the wind that had blown his hat away.
Across the canyon, silver in the sun,
the fuselage glinted. The wreck was ten years old,
two liners that had come together in broad day,
dropping their metal feathers,
and two tribes of travellers who settled then
where the wind told them to settle.

To that lost Indian tribe, who farmed this dry grandeur once,
they might have seemed to be surrogates of gods
(anything but gods, these downcast mortals,
anything but wrathful, they fell bemused
at various unfulfillments, at sheer bad luck)
as they descended, shorn of all human gear
and taking what they found: the shimmering desert air,
white water, the hot shale.
                And the hectoring solitude
that now made the rafters douse and romp and chatter,
a solitude that reverts to the subject of death
whenever the conversation of live things lags.

POEM

The swans on the river, a great
flotilla in the afternoon sun
in October again.

In a fantasy, Yeats saw himself appear
to Maud Gonne as a swan,
his plumage fanning his desire.

One October at Coole Park
he counted fifty-nine wild swans.
He flushed them into a legend.

Lover by lover is how he said they flew,
but one of them must have been without a mate.
Why did he not observe that?

We talk about Zeus and Leda and Yeats
as if they were real people, we identify constellations
as if they were drawn there on the night.

Cygnus and Castor & Pollux
are only ways of looking at
scatterings of starry matter,

a god putting on swan-flesh
to enter a mortal girl
is only a way of looking at love-trouble.

The violence and calm of these big fowl!
When I am not with you
I am always the fifty-ninth.

THE SEASONS' DIFFERENCE

Here on the warm strand, where a turquoise light
without horizon combs and breaks, menacing
only as love or morning menace
the man-made errors of the world,
I receive a contrary vision:
For an instant I seem to stand alone
under a lead sky, in late afternoon,
in winter. The grey will thicken soon
to snow, and I desire this vision
as one desires his own smell and person.
The mind waiting for snow is the true mind.
Numb tongue and lips speak for it clumsily
but turquoise baubles cannot distract it for long.

Before the thick-lipped winter-thinker
in me can explain, you explain. *Both,*
you call from where the sheer ocean
shelves off from a man's height, *Both,*
with the impatience of summer
and whatever is always between us.
As if to show me how to take a season
on its own terms, you ride a glass sea-slide
into the foamy shallows where I stand,
grey and stubborn as a snow-man.

FOR TWO LOVERS
IN THE YEAR 2075 IN
THE CANADIAN WOODS

If you have lips and forests,
you creatures years from now,
here are some lines to tell you
that we were among your trees
in extraordinary flesh
and ecstasy now gone,
and our tongues looked for each other
and after that for words.

If you have August moonrise
and bodies to undress,
here are some words we've left you
when we had had our say.
Put them beside your cummings,
if you still carry books,
not as sweet as Landor,
not as quick as Donne,
wrap them in still-warm clothing
beside your sleeping-bag
for when you want to speak.

These trees are stirred by ghosting,
not only ours but others'.
Enjoy the feathery presences,
no sadder than your own,
they gather from the past—
last August's moan and whisper,
an Indian brave and his maiden,

a French girl and her man—
the leaves renew the weavings
and lacings of the flesh.
Here is the sound of ours.

MEMOIRS

Even when he was a child, the Emperor
remembered, cartography had been a passion.
He had vexed his mother by turning carpets over
and drawing on the undersides in chalk
the map of Europe from memory or after his own heart.
Mountains and their defiles, rivers and plains,
rather than kingdoms, were what he said he drew.

The Empress-Mother, small by now and round,
her feet resting comfortably on the Aubusson
at Saint Cloud, said rather irritably, Maps?
Maps? We were much too poor in Corsica to have rugs.

GIVE AND TAKE

(Christmas, after a death in the family)

What are these presents   Look how many
have come unwrapped   & the stockings
tight with tangerines & kisses
& heavy Swiss things   deserved &
undeserved & deserved again
before you can open them   Look
they are stolen by little unwrappers
who whisper at dawn   who
come downstairs in their bed-clothes
to loot & grow older & us

Presence of love in this house
gifts of it   words of it
words for giving assent   about taking too
taking too much   Tell the children not to
Why not   tell ourselves not to
it is more blessed not to   but we take
naturally   we take to one another
wrapped in flesh tinsel & tissue   we are all
gaudy rejoicers in taking   two's   those two
we two   some alone   some alone

It's about time   & about love   both
this impatience to unwrap   to wrap
arms around airy expensive unholdable
things   Swiss chocolate kisses & pine
trees or spruce   one another
Often we're shiny & wanted
Tinsel is cheap   We believe it
It wouldn't glisten without eyes

No one in the whole world was ever bad
we lie   greedy or not   Hurry up   unwrap
this love is for you   where's mine
Hug the world now & thank it

Because over it hangs like our green wreath
a black wreath   a prescience
of days coming to some end
Not all spruce-smell & singing is gay
Some are not here

Boxes gape open   compartments of time
Is it nicely snowing outside this snug room
or do we stand suddenly in an autumn field
Who is the one in the box   Will God unwrap her
gladly & tell her the rest
after we've tied her up grassily
& told her goodnight   Lie still now
we've told her   God will be glad
at what we've thought of to bring him
He who has everything   sooner or later

It's hard giving people   Lucky is our habit
Are we lucky   still clutching here   losing
& trying to give back to the indian-giver
while the dark wreath reminds on the door
Just now in the early twilight
how dark the hemlock wreath
already unchristmassed
& these are not mechanical Swiss things
we are asked to rewrap & return
We do it as well as we can
but we're small thieves by nature   & keepers

In the autumn field where we left her
stands a distant insatiable relative
waiting to take what is his   to ease us
or torture us   which   into a box
where we'll lie still   still murmuring
give me   *love me*   smaller & smaller
asking in a voice of tiny unwrapping
astonishment   *mine*   *is it really for me*

STAGES

i

A child's contempt for his juniors:
how can a creature accept such helplessness?
(helplessness greater even than mine).

ii

A child's contempt for his juniors
yielding, with difficulty and, ah, crucially,
to the grown-up's fiction of childhood:
time of happy reliance on trustworthy others.

iii

Trustworthy others?

iv

The adult's acceptance of childhood as a metaphor.
Stoically we surround ourselves with children:
accidents of our joy, the embarrassment joy causes,
little memento mori's,
our likenesses, our helpless likenesses.
How they laugh, how they naturally laugh.
For a time they abide their ignorance.

v

For a time we abide ours.

vi

For the children's sake
we must not say so.

C

PARENTS

What it must be like to be an angel
or a squirrel, we can imagine sooner.

The last time we go to bed good,
they are there, lying about darkness.

They dandle us once too often,
these friends who become our enemies.

Suddenly one day, their juniors
are as old as we yearn to be.

They get wrinkles where it is better
smooth, odd coughs, and smells.

It is grotesque how they go on
loving us, we go on loving them.

The effrontery, barely imaginable,
of having caused us. And of how.

Their lives: surely
we can do better than that.

This goes on for a long time. Everything
they do is wrong, and the worst thing,

they all do it, is to die,
taking with them the last explanation,

how we came out of the wet sea
or wherever they got us from,

taking the last link
of that chain with them.

Father, mother, we cry, wrinkling,
to our uncomprehending children and grandchildren.

MY MOTHER'S LIFE

A woman neither young nor old, she moves
along the dark suburban street
swaddled against the night and cold
in a bright cloak. Only her face
and her small ankles are exposed
as she walks briskly towards some life she walks toward.
She is tired, and I think at this moment
she is expecting nothing. Not this. *Not this:*

a klieg light spots her from the sky
across the street. Out of the air it asks.
It asks something of the face she turns upward
to the supernatural light. I don't hear the question,
the illumination dazes the other senses.
And in the dream I watch the woman's face
as composure and surprise dispute its plainness.

I think she gives the right answer, before
the light dims, bluing, then purpling the retina.

IDEOGRAM

I am trying to describe to you a river at first light.
The water is glassy, under a scud of mist.
It is taking the color of the new sky
but the mist has something else in mind than pink—
a force of discoloration, it would have everything white.
On the far bank are serried low hills, tree-clusters,
occasionally the lights of a car.

This river I want you to see is being remembered.
I tell you this not to make us self-conscious
or conscious of words, but hoping to heighten
the peculiar vividness of a thing imagined.
I put no water-bird or craft on the surface:
the poem is absolutely quiet at about 5 a.m.
Rose-grey water slips away to left and right, silky,
upstream and downstream, just before sunrise,
just before we are called away,
you who don't know me, I who don't know you.

Soon it will be full light. We will blink this river away
and my talking to you, a stranger, as if I knew you,
as if our partaking a strange river at the edge of light
had been no impertinence—this will yield to another subject.
A river talked away, may be the new subject, or,
Mist burned off by the sun, an ancient, common figure,
a nearly dead metaphor, for enlightenment, and
it occurs to me now that someone may have already
accomplished this for you, hundreds of years ago,
someone deft with a brush, in China.

GRIEVANCES

Now and perpetually, over
the dark side of the earth
flows a tide of wakefulness
through chosen men and women,
the changing hostels of grievance,
which travels by night.

In Dublin a huge old man
is falling to sleep, having for hours
rehearsed words for tomorrow
to say to his shiftless nephew,
his sister's son, who's been making
the flat upstairs a brothel

while a tossing girl in Rio
abruptly turns on the light
and getting out of bed
puts on a flannel bathrobe
and goes to the typewriter.
I have forgiven you for the last time . . .

This is the after-edge of night.
Seen from far off, it's the last
dark segment before the purple band
that glows at the edge of the ball,
the edge of the planet that is
spinning again into sunlight.

Not thirty degrees east
the surly hosts are throwing off
the fit, or trying to, faced
with sun-cheer and bird-cheer,
the mindless smiles of dogs and children,
accumulating evidence of day.

Meanwhile and perpetually, these
hoboes make a sour clock of our globe.
Choosing you once or often,
or settling in, they pass
through your town each night
and have to have lodging.

For the life of me, I can't
turn one away. In the morning
they write on the fence by the door
in cyphers no man can erase:
this one mails the letters
or, *this one says the words.*

HERE AND THERE

for Sylvia Shelly

Whose spirit is this? we said, because we knew
It was the spirit that we sought and knew
That we should ask this often as she sang.

  "The Idea of Order at Key West" / Wallace Stevens

i

Here in the north, a cold grey morning
does not deter the still-mating birds:
two orioles, a wood-thrush? I'm not good
at this quick argot, so particular
but sounding all alike to a foreigner.
There's no heat in the house of course in May
unless I light a fire. Stevens
I think would have lighted one today
and, comfortable with my betters, I do too.

ii

There in Key West, the singer lies asleep,
perhaps under a fan, after playing late
at the café. They kept her playing and singing
by the edge of the warm gulf
(after she'd watched the sun drop into it,
staying to cup Hesperus in her small hands
against the wind that rises suddenly then,
until his flame caught)—they wouldn't let her stop
at one o'clock. Now the current
runs past the island very fast
as if in panic. But the trees flower
calmly in the heat outside her house.

iii

Now there are whole mindfulls of climate
in Connecticut and Florida, ideas
of moisture and drought, cold and hot—
living and dead, for that matter.
Think of how many ideas are dancing in pairs.
The idea of Wallace Stevens dancing alone
is picked up and held in mind briefly,
here and there, like a bird-call. What
is the difference between ourselves and ghosts?
Only that we move awkwardly through the air.

iv

While my cold birds chirrup—I dare not say mindlessly—
in Connecticut, and the crackling on the hearth
begins to warm me, I hear as well
the tart music of last night in the piano bar
glassed in from the green-lighted water off Key West,
the laughter struck with certain resonances
that is Sylvia's particular call,
though I think she is still asleep,
perhaps with a ceiling fan turning slowly
above her bed, between two ideas, a gulf and an ocean.

REMEMBERING ROBERT LOWELL

The message you brought back again and again
from the dark brink had the glitter of truth.
From the beginning, you told it as memoir:
even though you didn't cause it,
the memoirs said of the trouble they recounted,
it was always your familiar when it came.

Your language moved slowly towards our language
until we saw that we were all immigrants—
had perhaps been shipped as convicts—
from the land of your reluctant indictment,
a land of our consent, if not of our doing.

It was your jokes and stories, when you were alive,
the wry imitations and the bad boy's laugh,
that roped us from the brink you led us to.
We will miss that laughter, left to the glittering poems,
the raw gist of things.

To punish the bearer of evil tidings
it is our custom to ask his blessing.
This you gave. It dawns on each of us separately now
what this entails.

DREAMS OF SUICIDE

(In sorrowful memory of Ernest Hemingway,
Sylvia Plath, and John Berryman)

i

I reach for the awkward shotgun not to disarm
you, but to feel the metal horn,
furred with the downy membrane of dream.
More surely than the unicorn,
you are the mythical beast.

ii

Or I am sniffing an oven. On all fours
I am imitating a totemic animal
but she is not my totem or the totem
of my people, this is not my magic oven.

iii

If I hold you tight by the ankles,
still you fly upward from the iron railing.
Your father made these wings,
after he made his own, and now from beyond
he tells you *fly down*, in the voice
my own father might say *walk, boy.*

IN LOVING MEMORY OF
THE LATE AUTHOR
OF DREAM SONGS

Friends making off ahead of time
on their own, I call that willful, John,
but that's not judgment, only argument
such as we've had before.
I watch a shaky man climb
a cast-iron railing in my head, on
a Mississippi bluff, though I had meant
to dissuade him. I call out, and he doesn't hear.

"Fantastic! Fantastic! Thank thee, dear Lord"
is what you said we were to write on your stone,
but you go down without so much as a note.
Did you wave jauntily, like the German ace
in a silent film, to a passer-by, as the paper said?
We have to understand how you got
from here to there, a hundred feet straight down.
Though you had told us and told us,
and how it would be underground
and how it would be for us left here,
who could have plotted that swift chute
from the late height of your prizes?
For all your indignation, your voice
was part howl only, part of it was caress.
Adorable was a word you threw around,
fastidious John of the gross disguises,
and *despair* was another: "this work of almost despair."

Morale is what I think about all the time
now, what hopeful men and women can say and do.
But having to speak for you, I can't
lie. "Let his giant faults appear, as sent
together with his virtues down," the song says.
It says suicide is a crime
and that wives and children deserve better than this.
None of us deserved, of course, you.

Do we wave back now, or what do we do?
You were never reluctant to instruct.
I do what's in character, I look for things
to praise on the river banks and I praise them.
We are all relicts, of some great joy, wearing black,
but this book is full of marvelous songs.
Don't let us contract your dread recidivism
and start falling from our own iron railings.
Wave from the fat book again, make us wave back.

JOHN AND ANNE

I would call the subject of Anne Frank's Diary even more mysterious than St. Augustine's, and describe it as: the conversion of a child into a person. . . . It took place under very special circumstances which—let us now conclude as she concluded—though superficially unfavorable, were in fact highly favorable to it; she was forced to mature, in order to survive; the hardest challenge, let's say, that a person can face without defeat is the best for him.

"The Development of Anne Frank" / John Berryman

Are you grown up now, John, now that it's over?
Do you sit around sober and peaceful these days,
listening to the big people's palaver,
nobody interrupting, nobody famished for praise?

(We have to fable some such place of good talk
 —Nobody listens to me, the child would shout—
because we ourselves remain shrill little folk:
there must be somewhere we'll hear each other out.)

Do you engage your friends in the ghostly scene
with decorum you could only parody as a man:
Anne Bradstreet and the Governor, St. Augustine,
Jarrell, and this other, child-woman Anne?

It was a long time coming, this quiet,
this hard adulthood, after tantrums of enquiry.
Nobody answers my questions, the child would shout.
You went from the one bottle to the other, thirsty.

"The hardest challenge, let's say, that a person can face
without defeat is the best for him." She could weep
at Auschwitz for the naked gypsy girls gassed in that place.
Dying at Belsen, she helped you to grow up.

DYING AWAY

(Homage to Sigmund Freud)

"Toward the person who has died
we adopt a special attitude:
something like admiration
for someone who has accomplished
a very difficult task," he said,

and now hospitals and rest-homes
are filled with heroes and heroines
in smocks, at their out-sized, unwonted tasks,
now the second date on tombstones is a saint's day
and there is no craven in any graveyard,

no malingerer there, no trivial person.
It is you and I, still milling around,
who evade our callings, incestuous
in our love for the enduring trees and the snowfall,
for brook-noise and coins, songs, appetites.

And with the one we love most,
the mated one we lose track of ourselves in—
who's giving, who's taking that fleshy pleasure?—
we call those calmings-away, those ecstasies
dyings, we see them as diligent rehearsals.

The love of living disturbs me,
I am wracked like a puritan by eros and health,
almost undone by brotherhood, rages
of happiness seize me, the world, the fair world,
and I call on the name of the dark healer, Freud.

His appetites, songs, orgasms died away,
his young brother, his daughter, his huge father,
until he saw that the *aim* of life was death.
But a man cannot learn heroism from another,
he owes the world some death of his own invention.

Then he said, "My dear Schur, you certainly remember
our first talk. You promised me then not to forsake me
when my time came. Now it is nothing but torture
and makes no sense any more."
Schur gave him two centigrams of morphine.

At what cost he said it, so diligent of life,
so curious, we can't guess
who are still his conjurings. He told us
it is impossible to imagine our own deaths,
he told us, this may be the secret of heroism.

THE REVENANT

Kilgore Trout owned a parakeet named Bill. . . . Trout sneered and muttered to his parakeet about the end of the world.

"Any time now," he would say. "And high time, too."

It was Trout's theory that the atmosphere would become unbreathable soon.

Trout supposed that when the atmosphere became poisonous, Bill would keel over a few minutes before Trout did. He would kid Bill about that. "How's the old respiration, Bill?" he'd say, or, "Seems like you've got a touch of the old emphysema, Bill," or, "We never discussed what kind of a funeral you want, Bill. You never even told me what your religion is." And so on.

He told Bill that humanity deserved to die horribly, since it had behaved so cruelly and wastefully on a planet so sweet. "We're all Heliogabalus, Bill," he would say. This was the name of a Roman emperor who had a sculptor make a hollow, life-size iron bull with a door on it. The door could be locked from the outside. The bull's mouth was open. That was the only other opening to the outside.

Heliogabalus would have a human being put into the bull through the door, and the door would be locked. And sounds the human being made in there would have to come out of the mouth of the bull. Heliogabalus would have guests in for a nice party, with plenty of food and wine and beautiful women and pretty boys —and Heliogabalus would have a servant light kindling. The kindling was under dry firewood—which was under the bull.

Breakfast of Champions / Kurt Vonnegut

I am a spirit now. After that death,
I died in great pain only once, a cancer
in my stomach the size of a melon,
and with morphine I could keep silence.
Sometimes when the grandchildren shouted at play
outside the house, I felt the passion to shout too,
but remembered the lesson.

When they put me inside the clanking belly
I understood what I had to do, I had
simply to keep quiet. As it grew hot
I thrashed my arms and legs as quietly as I could,
the way a deaf-mute might scream. The noise
of the fire was enough to keep him from hearing
my scrabbling, and I was careful.
Denied the expression of screams, my body
danced out its message. In my mind
I could see the jowly emperor's pain.
"Last time, it bellowed as if in orgasm,"
he shouted to the disappointed guests,
some of them already lost in drink or love-making.

I gained two stages of progress by that dance
but Heliogabalus did not profit from my show
of continence, could not learn anything
from his iron beast, speaking a blessed silence.
He was not elevated by that existence.

1976

CROSSING OVER

It was now early spring, and the river was swollen and turbulent; great cakes of floating ice were swinging heavily to and fro in the turbid waters. Owing to a peculiar form of the shore, on the Kentucky side, the land bending far out into the water, the ice had been lodged and detained in great quantities, and the narrow channel which swept round the bend was full of ice, piled one cake over another, thus forming a temporary barrier to the descending ice, which lodged, and formed a great undulating raft.... Eliza stood, for a moment, contemplating this unfavorable aspect of things.

> Uncle Tom's Cabin (Chapter VII, "The
> Mother's Struggle") / Harriet Beecher Stowe

That's what love is like. The whole river
is melting. We skim along in great peril,

having to move faster than ice goes under
and still find foothold in the soft floe.

We are one another's floe. Each displaces the weight
of his own need. I am fat as a bloodhound,

hold me up. I won't hurt you. Though I bay,
I would swim with you on my back until the cold

seeped into my heart. We are committed, we
are going across this river willy-nilly.

No one, black or white, is free in Kentucky,
old gravity owns everybody. We're weighty.

I contemplate this unfavorable aspect of things.
Where is something solid? Only you and me.

Has anyone ever been to Ohio?
Do the people there stand firmly on icebergs?

Here all we have is love, a great undulating
raft, melting steadily. We go out on it

anyhow. I love you, I love this fool's walk.
The thing we have to learn is how to walk light.

NOT BOTH

> *. . . I sleep on. And again*
> *Old Zack, pore ole white-trash—croker sack dragging—*
> *Is out to scrounge coal off the L & N tracks.*
> *Old Mag at it too, face knobby, eyes bleared,*
> *Mouth dribbling with snuff, skirts swinging*
> *Above the old brogan she's fixed for her clubfoot,*
> *And dragging her own sack for coal.*
> *They don't hear the whistle. Or Zack's*
> *Just stubborn, born democrat, knowing damned well*
> *That the coal, it is his, and by rights.*
> *Then the whistle again, in outrage and anguish.*
>
> *And now I wake up, or not. If I don't*
> *It blows on like hell, brakes screaming,*
> *And Mag, of a sudden, is down. The brogan she wears*
> *For the clubfoot, it looks like it's caught*
> *In a switch-V—the coal chute starts here.*
> *And I stand in a weedy ditch, my butterfly*
> *Net in my hand, my chloroform jar,*
> *Mount box, and canteen strung on me—and Zack,*
> *He keeps pulling. She's up. Zack bends at the brogan.*
> *The whistle goes wild. Brakes scream. I stare.*
>
> *Zack's up, foot's out! Or is it? A second she's standing,*
> *Then down—now over both rails—*
> *Down for good, and the last*
> *Thing I see is his hands out. To grab her, I reckoned.*

"Recollection in Upper Ontario" / Robert Penn Warren

The club-footed woman was mangled by the train.
Her husband was trying to free her foot from the switch-V
or he was holding her foot there so the train would kill her.

The tall girl and her over-handsome brother
who lived those years together in the city
while she practiced harpsichord and he the law,
till one day he married a rich woman, and she,
months later, an older man, a lawyer—
they were lovers those seven years, or they weren't.

The woman who sailed her dinghy out in the Bay
in the fall blow—autumn is for beginnings—
and was found miles from the zig-zagging sailboat
that she knew like a husband—either she sought
a way to drown or the Chesapeake taught her, not both.

Either before I die I'll falter and tell
the strange secret I was given once as a token
or I'll manage to carry it with me.

Somebody knows or nobody knows these answers.

One of those two appalling things is true too.

REM SLEEP

The first indication that sleep might be more than a unitary state occurred when several researchers, Nathaniel Klietman, Eugene Aserinsky, and William Dement, noted the occurrence of rapid eye movements at various intervals during a night's sleep. As a result of these findings, sleep was divided into two major categories: rapid-eye-movement, REM sleep, and an independent stage of nonrapid-eye-movement or NREM sleep. . . . Considerable interest has focused on REM sleep since it was noted that dream recall frequently followed awakening from this sleep phase.

McGraw-Hill Encyclopedia of Science & Technology

I direct that my body not be buried until such time as it shows signs of decomposition. I mention this because during my illness there have already been moments of deathly numbness when my heart and pulse stopped beating.

Last Will and Testament / N. V. Gogol

*"They've stolen my linen from under my frock coat.
There's a draft through a crack. But there's no way to get through it.*

*Even Christ suffered less
before waking up in the grave!"
The subterranean cry did not shake the depths.
Two men had a drink on the grave.
We enjoy funerals just as
you enjoy hearing how Gogol was buried.*

*Unseal his coffin freezing in the snow.
Gogol, writhing, lies on his side.
His twisted toenail has torn the lining in his boot.*

*"The Interment of Nicolai Vasilich Gogol" / Andrei Voznesensky,
translated by Vera Dunham and F. W. Tjalsma*

What are the two poor children thinking there,
thrashing nightly behind my lids,
trapped behind the soft eyelids like little Gogols?

"Do not bury us," they spell out every day
in colored crayons, "until you're sure we're dead,
until our orbs show signs of discoloration."

Can they communicate there, the two inseparables?
Or at that distance apart does the flesh muffle sound,
the tamped cells stifle their cries like rained-on soil?

And what kind of instinct do you call the blind health
that bids them forget, every blessed morning,
the terrible entombment?

Sometimes I hear one eye say to another
in sing-song, making an old-country joke of it,
"What an unlucky dream I dreamt last night. If I
                                believed in dreams. . . ."

OF KINDNESS

And the behavior released in us, by such confrontations, is, essentially,
a surprised affection. . . . Maybe altruism is our most primitive attribute.

　　　　　　　　The Medusa and the Snail　/　Lewis Thomas

Where people live on earth there is a kind
of water-table, a reservoir that rises and falls,
man-made, mysterious, our chemistry and purpose.
The fluid it holds is sweet to us,
we've caught it over and over
the way the thirsty ocean catches the rain.
This is the tribe's own drink. It flows
over populated land like history. It stands
in cisterns, rare as fortunate history.

There's never quite enough to slake us all.
We come to the well-head daily and thirsty.
Daily and thirsty we're given the chance to drink
and to draw water—to carry some, uphill,
in leather buckets, on a pole across our shoulders
or on the flanks of burros, in the hot sun,
where dust is the general rule. We carry it,
and at the well-head we wolf some down.

Does this wetness buoy us, like the bucket
of water that's all it takes to float a warship?
Like the cup of blood that's called grace?
At the fountain of Aesculapius (I've heard this story)
halfway up a mountain in the Aegean,
an unthinking traveller washed his sweat away
in the spring's sweet marble trough,
so that the little accidental tribe
he had climbed with knew angry drought;
while elsewhere at that moment,
attentive on the desert of her dying,

an old Spanish woman drew,
from a secret rivulet she knew,
laughter that doused her folk with crystal
that they could drink and go across without her.

Birds and the nearer animals are always
chiding us to be attentive to this flux. Swallows
riffling the surface of a pond
are cousins and reminders of our kind.

This is most of what is known about kindness
among our dry kind.

TRELAWNY'S DREAM

Edward John Trelawny, who is imagined to speak the following lines in his late middle age, survived his friend Shelley by almost sixty years, and lies beside him in the Protestant Cemetery in Rome. He seems to have met no man or woman in a long life whom he could marvel at and love as he did Shelley. Trelawny had intended to convoy the poet and Edward Williams (and a cabin-boy Charles Vivian) when they sailed the *Ariel* out of Leghorn into the storm that drowned them, but Lord Byron's yacht, which he was commanding, was detained at the last minute by port authorities. He cremated the remains of his friends, and recovered the little boat, which appeared to have been run down by a larger vessel, though the violent squall into which the *Ariel* disappeared would have been enough to founder the keel-heavy boat which Trelawny himself had unwisely designed for the novice Shelley.

W.M.

The dark illumination of a storm
and water-noise, chuckling along the hull
as the craft runs tight before it.
Sometimes Shelley's laughter wakes me here,
unafraid, as he was the day he dove
into water for the first time, a wooded pool
on the Arno, and lay like a conger eel
on the bottom—"where truth lies," he said—
until I hauled him up.

But oftener the dream insists on all,
insists on retelling all.
                              Ned Williams is the first
to see the peril of the squall. His shout
to lower sail scares the deck-boy wide-eyed
and cuts off Shelley's watery merriment.
The big wind strokes the cat-boat like a kitten.
Riding the slate-grey hillocks, she is dragged
by the jib Ned Williams leaves to keep her head.
The kitten knows the wind is a madman's hand
and the bay a madman's lap.
As she scuds helpless, only the cockney boy
Charles Vivian and I, a dreamer and a child,
see the felucca loom abeam. Her wet lateen
ballooning in the squall, she cuts across
wind and seas in a wild tack, she is on us.
The beaked prow wrenches the little cabin
from the deck, tosses the poet slowly to the air—
he pockets his book, he waves to me and smiles—
then to his opposite element,

light going into darkness, gold into lead.
The felucca veers and passes, a glimpse of a face
sly with horror on her deck. I watch our brave
sailor boy stifle his cry of knowledge
as the boat takes fatal water, then Ned's stricken face,
scanning the basalt waves
for what will never be seen again except in dreams.

All this was a long time ago, I remember.
None of them was drowned except me
whom a commotion of years washes over.
They hail me from the dream, they call an old man
to come aboard, these youths on an azure bay.
The waters may keep the dead, as the earth may,
and fire and air. But dream is my element.
Though I am still a strong swimmer
I can feel this channel widen as I swim.

EXAMPLES OF CREATED SYSTEMS

i.   the stars

We look out at them on clear nights, thrilled
rather than comforted—brilliance and
distance put us in mind of our
own burnings and losses. And then who
flung them there, in a sowing motion
suggesting that random is beautiful?

ii.   archipelagoes

Or again, the islands that the old
cartographers, triangulating
their first glimpses of bays and peaks, set
down, and which the rich traveller, from
a high winter chair, chooses among
today—chains of jade thrown across the
torso of the sea-mother, herself
casually composed.

iii.   work camps and prisons

                    The homeless
Solzhenitsyn, looking at Russia,
saw a configuration of camps
spotting his homeland, "ports" where men
and women were forced to act out
the birth-throes of volcanic islands,

the coral patience of reefs, before
a "ship," a prison train, bore them down
that terrible archipelago
conceived and made by men like ourselves.

iv.   those we love

Incorrigibly (it is our nature)
when we look at a map we look for
the towns and valleys and waterways
where loved people constellate, some of
them from our blood, some from our own loins.
This fair scattering of matter is
all we will know of creation, at
first hand. We flung it there, in a learned
gesture of sowing—random, lovely.

A NOTE ABOUT THE AUTHOR

*William Meredith was born in New York City in 1919, was graduated from
Princeton in 1940, and served as a naval aviator during the Second World War.
His first book of poems,* Love Letter from an Impossible Land, *was chosen by
Archibald MacLeish, in 1944, for the Yale Series of Younger Poets; the title
poem had been written the year before, in the Aleutian Islands;* Ships and Other
Figures, *his second book of verse, was published in Princeton in 1948.* The
Open Sea *(1958),* The Wreck of the Thresher *(1964),* Earth Walk: New & Selected
Poems *(1970), and* Hazard, the Painter *(1975) were each published by Knopf.*

William Meredith has won three of Poetry's *annual prizes, and a grant from
and the Loines Award from the National Academy of Arts and Letters, of which
he became a member in 1968. Since 1964 he has been a chancellor of the
Academy of American Poets, and from 1978 through 1980 he has been the
Consultant in Poetry to the Library of Congress. Mr. Meredith has taught
at Princeton, the University of Hawaii, Middlebury College, Breadloaf, and
Carnegie-Mellon University, but has been primarily associated with
Connecticut College since 1955.*

A NOTE ABOUT THE TYPE

The text of this book was set in Olympus, *a film version of* Trump Mediaeval.
Designed by Professor Georg Trump in the mid-1950s, Trump Mediaeval *was cut
and cast by the C. E. Weber Typefoundry of Stuttgart, West Germany. The roman
letterforms are based on classical prototypes, but Professor Trump has imbued
them with his own unmistakable style. The italic letterforms, unlike those of
so many other typefaces, are closely related to their roman counterparts. The
result is a truly contemporary type, notable both for its legibility and versatility.*

*This book was composed by Superior Printing, Champaign, Illinois, and printed
and bound by American Book–Stratford Press, Saddle Brook, New Jersey.*

Designed by Margaret M. Wagner